JEWS WHO HELPED

SETTLE THE WILD WEST

JEWS WHO HELPED SETTLE THE WILD WEST

Edwin M. Radin

Paperback ISBN: 978-1-63337-426-3
E-book ISBN: 978-1-63337-427-0

Printed in the United States of America

1 3 5 7 9 10 8 6 4 2

Contents

AUTHOR'S NOTE

I HAD JUST FINISHED MY BOOK *Gersham and the Golem* and began thinking about my next book. Writing *Gersham and the Golem* was fun to write and put together and used a lot of my imagination which made the story, exciting and kept you on the edge of your seat. My readers loved the book and kept asking me what my next project would be. In my mind there were lots of Judaic subjects I could write about. But the Wild West has always been a favorite subject of mine. As I looked around at libraries and on-line, I could not find one book on Jewish settlers in the Old West. I found articles and a few short stories. However, there had to be more. So, I dug in and researched the Jewish people who helped settle the west. I was amazed at all the different characters and stories I found. The more research, the more excited I became.

There were gunfighters, lawmen, and entrepreneurs. There were brave women who helped run their Jewish homes and served as mid wives and teachers. The hospitality industry was founded to better serve the people when they traveled to and from the west by railroad. There were Jews who traded with and helped the Indian tribes remain in their territories. And there were men who served in government.

I have put together stories and pictures of the Jewish people who immigrated to the United States and travelled west looking to better their lives.

I invite you to pick up a copy of my book and enjoy the many wonderful people and stories they have to tell. And hopefully you'll be as fascinated with Jews who settled the Wild West. Thank you and enjoy. Happy reading.

EDWIN M. RADIN

Dedicated to my family and the Jewish people who immigrated to the United States to help build their future and ours.

Jews who Helped Settle the Wild West

Frederick Henry Harvey

MANY JEWS HELPED TAME THE WILD WEST. One of the most popular Jewish figures was Mr. Frederick Henry Harvey. Mr. Harvey was the founding father of the American hospitality industry. He was also famous for his Harvey Girls, who provided services to the patrons who visited his establishments.

Mr. Harvey was born June 27, 1835 in London, England. At the age of seventeen, Harvey immigrated from Liverpool, England, to the United States and took a job as a dishwasher/busboy at a popular New York City restaurant called Smith and McNells. He quickly learned the restaurant business from the owners Henry Smith and T.R. McNell. He was taught about the importance of quality service, fresh ingredients, and a firm handshake to end the deal. Harvey quickly moved up the company ladder to waiter and then line cook.

After eighteen months, Harvey moved to New Orleans. After surviving a sickness, he then moved to St. Louis, Missouri. He got a job in a jewelry store. It was then he met his wife and married her and had six children.

Harvey was very successful selling jewelry. However, he felt compelled to return to the food industry. He and a partner started a small café and turned it into a very profitable business. However, with the start of the Civil War, his partner took all the money and left town.

After the closing of the café, Harvey began working for the Hannibal and St. Louis Railroad, climbing up the ranks quickly, and was then transferred to Leavenworth, Kansas, which became his permanent home.

Mr. Harvey frequently traveled while working for the railroad and was very dissatisfied with the food that was served to the travelers.

In 1876, Harvey began a new partnership with the Santa Fe Railroad and struck a deal with Charles Morse, the superintendent of the Atchison, Topeka, and Santa Fe railroad. Harvey opened up eating houses along the railroad. Mr. Morse did not charge him any rent, and again, they sealed the deal with a handshake. At the peak of business, there were eighty-four Harvey Houses which catered to the wealthy and the middle-class tourists and passengers. Mr. Harvey was becoming known as "The Civilizer of the West."

Mr. Harvey also boosted his eateries with the addition of the Harvey Girls. Mr. Harvey had experienced poor service and unfriendly people in his travels and decided he would hire women who had personality and a great sense of humor. He posted job openings through the telegraph and across the United States territory. He wanted his girls to be between eighteen and thirty years old. Their job was to wait on his customers and serve their food in a timely fashion. Mr. Harvey would not allow the girls to marry until they had worked for him one year. He also gave them free housing in a place right next to his restaurants. The oldest of the girls or senior girl was the supervisor of the house and enforced curfews and chaperoned male visits. Roughly about five thousand Harvey

girls moved out west to work for Mr. Harvey and eventually got married and helped grow the population of the west.

Mr. Harvey remained the head of his business through the year of 1900. He, then, retired and passed on the restaurants to his sons and grandsons until the business was finally sold in 1968.

Mr. Harvey passed away on February 9, 1901 in Leavenworth, Kansas, from intestinal cancer. When he passed, there were forty-seven restaurants, fifteen hotels, and thirty dining cars operating on the Santa Fe railway. Mr. Harvey was best known as "The father of hospitality and the American service industry."

KANSAS TO NEW MEXICO

TWO LESSER KNOWN JEWS who started working for Fred Harvey were David Benjamin and Herman Schweizer. They were the first prominent Jews to do business all over the western United States. Mr. Benjamin was a very serious-minded British Jew with a roundish body and wire-rimmed glasses with a trim mustache.

Mr. Benjamin worked as a bank teller in Leavenworth, Kansas, in the 1870s and was hired by Fred Harvey to run the day-to-day operations of his Kansas-City-based hospitality empire. Under Mr. Benjamin, the empire grew to include over sixty trackside dining rooms, twenty-five hotels, a huge cattle ranch, three large dairy and poultry farms, and a beverage facility that had the only license in town to bottle its own Coca Cola. He managed a staff of over seven thousand employees in eighty different locations, so rigid systems had to be put in place. (Remember there were no telephones as of yet, so it was hard to communicate unless they wanted to use Western Union telegraph which was very costly at the time.) Mr. Benjamin also became a mentor to Mr. Harvey's son, Ford, so that he'd be able to take over the business when the time came.

Mr. Benjamin had four siblings. His brother Alfred lived with him and ran a large furniture company. Alfred also ran the UJC (United Jewish Charities) in Kansas City, Missouri, for eighteen years and was known to give half of his salary to charity. He was known as a real philanthropist.

David also worked with Alfred at the UJC and often partnered with local Catholic charities where Ford Harvey and his wife, Judy, were leaders. All were active in the YM-YWHA (Young Mens-Young Women's Hebrew Association) movement which lead to the creation of Jewish community centers, which served as places for Jews to go and served as a safe-haven.

Another Benjamin brother was Harry who also worked for Fred Harvey. He helped his sister Fannie open one of the country's first Jewish summer camps for needy immigrant children. In 1907 the camp was given the name Bittersweet Camp.

David Benjamin once said, "I try to follow the teachings of Judaism by helping anyone who needs help, Jewish or not.

His partner, Herman Schweizer, was a short stocky gentleman with a bald head who loved to smoke cigars. He was a German immigrant who started selling oranges on the Santa Fe trains until he became the manager of the Harvey House in Gallop, New

Mexico. Schweizer met Mr. Benjamin on one of the trains heading west and happened to sell him some of the finest oranges for his restaurant, and the two became fast friends. Mr. Benjamin offered Mr. Schweizer a job and he gladly accepted.

Besides running a restaurant, Mr. Schweizer loved riding on horseback and rode to nearby Navajo trading posts and villages to acquire blankets, pottery, and jewelry. Schweizer had an eye for beautiful artwork and enticing Indian jewelry. However, the tourists wanted lighter and cheaper pieces, so during his travels he bought up lots of turquoise and thinner silver to sell to the craftsmen to make rings and earrings. He was the driving force behind the beautiful Native American artwork serving all the major museums and private collectors. He bought every collection he could find, many from the Jewish merchants. Herman kept some of the less expensive artwork to put up in some of the Harvey Houses, so the tourists who came in for a meal could enjoy the art as well. This art fueled a growing interest in the native culture.

As Herman Schweizer got older, he became much more active in the Jewish community where he lived in Albuquerque, New Mexico. He was active with the local chapter of B'nai Brith and the Reform Congregation of Temple Albert. Mr. Schweizer died in 1925.

JULIUS MEIER

JULIUS MEIER was born in Portland, Oregon, on December 31, 1874. After graduating with a law degree from the University of Oregon in 1895 Julius became a general manager of his family's department store and led the company through a time of substantial revenue growth in 1910. Then four years later, he purchased the Columbia River estate that came to be known as Menucha, their family retreat where they entertained a lot of prominent friends and diplomats including Herbert Hoover and Franklin D. Roosevelt.

Meier was very active in his community providing leadership and financial help for the foundation of the Zionist Society of Oregon in 1901, and then in 1905 he gave financial support for the Lewis and Clark Exposition.

He entered politics when his friend and law partner George Joseph, the Republican candidate for governor, passed away due to a heart attack in 1930. Because the Republican party chose another candidate with different ideas about how the state should be governed, Meier decided to run as an independent candidate. Meier won the election with more votes than his two opponents combined.

Meier served as Oregon's governor from 1931–1935 during the darkest years of the Great Depression. He was forced to cut many state services including higher education in order to fix the budget deficit. He also promoted relief programs to ease the effects of unemployment. He is also known for his advocacy of old-age pensions and public power and for creating the Oregon State Police, the Liquor Control Commission, and the State Board of Agriculture. He fought for the maintenance of the state forests, beautification and cleaning of the highways, and protection of the beaches.

He did not seek a second term due to health concerns and retired to Menucha, where he died of a heart attack on July 14, 1937.

SOLOMON BIBO

ANOTHER JEWISH SETTLER was Solomon Bibo. He was born on July 15, 1853 in Brakel, Germany. His family came to Santa Fe, New Mexico, in 1869. His father was a cantor.

Solomon began trading with the Acoma tribe and became very close friends with them. Solomon traded furs, pots and pans, and turquoise jewelry with the tribe. He represented the tribe in property disputes with the federal government. He eventually married an Acoma woman.

In 1885, he became the tribe's chief. As chief, Solomon introduced a number of reforms persuading his tribe to establish the settlement in a more convenient location, introduced more modern ways to help their agriculture, and set up a school for Acoma children. After serving as their chief, Solomon moved his family to San Francisco, California, to live in a more Jewish environment and give his children a greater exposure to a Jewish life and education. Solomon Bibo passed away on May 4, 1934.

LOEB (LEVI) STRAUSS
SAN FRANCISCO, CALIFORNIA

IN 1853, a Jewish settler named Loeb (Levi) Strauss came to San Francisco with a dream to sell supplies to the miners. He came with lots of canvas to make tents for them. But soon after, he learned that the miners needed pants, not tents. The miners were always down on their hands and knees and ripped holes in the knee area of their pants. Levi Strauss dyed his canvas blue and made the first jeans with reinforced knees. He called his pants Levi's. The miners loved the jeans, and Mr. Strauss was on his way to riches making Levi's blue jeans. His jeans were so popular that cowboys, wranglers, ranchers, and just about everyone was wearing them.

Nineteen years later in 1872, a friend of his named Jacob Davis came to town and spoke to him about a unique method of reinforcing pants with metal rivets. This was a fantastic idea, and Jacob and Levi applied for a patent together. Upon receiving the patent, they began to manufacture rugged cotton pants with reinforced copper rivets at the stress points, and Levi's jeans became a staple piece of clothing for everyone to wear.

Levi Strauss was also very active in San Francisco's first synagogue as well as other Jewish institutions. He died in 1902 and divided his fortune between the Pacific Hebrew Orphan Home, the Hebrew Board of Relief, and started a scholarship at the University of California, Berkeley, which still continues to help students today.

SIMON BAMBERGER

SIMON BAMBERGER became the fourth governor for the state of Utah in 1917 and served until 1921. Simon had the distinction of being the first non-Mormon, the first Democrat, as well as the first and only Jew to hold this position in Utah.

Simon was born in Hesse-Darmstadt, Germany, in 1845. He came to America at fourteen years old looking to make his fortune. He came to New York and then departed for Cincinnati by train. He missed his transfer in Columbus, Ohio, and got off at the next stop in Indianapolis, Indiana, where he had family. He worked in Indianapolis until the Civil War ended.

His brother Herman migrated to the States shortly after Simon and the two of them moved to St. Louis, Missouri, and became clothing manufacturers. While Simon was in Wyoming on business, he learned from his brother that the manufacturing business had failed. Simon decided to travel on to the state of Utah, where he purchased a half interest in a small hotel in Ogden. But soon after, smallpox broke out and created an epidemic. He then went to Salt Lake City. In his own words Simon said,

"Soon thereafter an epidemic of smallpox broke out and the Union Pacific passengers were not permitted to come up to the town, so I gave up. I took the Utah Central to Salt Lake City and there I bought the Delmonico Hotel, and renamed it 'The White House,' in partnership with B. Cohen of Ogden."

The hotel flourished.

In 1872, Simon purchased an interest in a silver mine which by 1874 made him a very wealthy man. However, he had no thoughts of retiring. Two years later he raised a million dollars to construct a railroad to some coal mines in northern Utah in which he invested. Simon then built a second rail line to some smaller towns on the outskirts of Salt Lake City. Unfortunately, there was so much competition with the railroads that Simon had lost a lot of his fortune.

In the year 1910, Simon helped establish a Jewish agricultural colony in Clarion, Utah. Unfortunately, in 1913, when the immigrant farmers went bankrupt, Simon could not raise the funds to save the colony, and it folded in 1915.

Simon's Mormon friends had noted his civic mindedness and urged him to run for governor. Despite being a Democrat, Simon's policies were very much aligned to those of Teddy Roosevelt of the Republican Party. He worked to balance the budget, create a public utilities commission to regulate the price of electricity and gas, and banned gifts to public officials by the utility companies. Simon also created a state department of public health, worked on water conservation, and advocated for a longer school year. He also developed workers' compensation and supported prohibition. Most of his platforms were voted into law.

Simon Bamberger passed away on October 6, 1926. He was buried in the cemetery of Congregation B'nai Israel, the first synagogue in Salt Lake City, Utah.

BOISE, IDAHO
MOSES ALEXANDER

MOSES ALEXANDER was born on November 13, 1853 in Obrigheim, Germany, and became the second elected Jewish governor of Idaho from 1915–1919. He remains the state of Idaho's only Jewish governor

Moses came to the United States in 1867 and settled in New York City. He then migrated to Missouri where his cousin owned a clothing store. He showed a real talent for the business and was promoted and made a partner in 1874. In 1876, Moses married Helena Kaestner, a Christian immigrant from Germany who later converted to Judaism.

While in Missouri, Moses became very interested in politics, especially the ideas of the Democratic Party. In 1886, he was elected to the Chillicothe, Missouri City Council. By 1887, he was elected mayor of Chillicothe and served two terms.

By 1891, Moses left Missouri with the idea of moving to Alaska. However, a stop along the way in Boise, Idaho, changed all that. Moses stopped in Boise to research its investment opportunities. While there, he fell in love with the city of Boise and decided to settle there. In July that same year, he opened the first of many clothing stores called Alexander's. His stores were very profitable.

Then by 1895, Moses and other Jews in Boise got together to build Ahavath Beth Israel Synagogue, the first Jewish synagogue in Idaho. The building took one year to complete and is still in use today. It's the oldest synagogue west of the Mississippi River.

Moses was elected mayor of Boise in 1897 and served two years and chose not to run for re-election. However, by 1901, he was elected for another term. During his term as mayor, the Boise volunteer fire department was re-organized into a professional department, hiring permanent firefighters ready to protect the city. He also passed laws to enforce anti-gambling.

In 1914, Moses entered the governor's race on a platform that supported prohibition of alcohol and limited spending by the government. He won the election, becoming the first Jew to take office of governor in a U.S. state. He was a popular leader and went on to serve another two-year term.

Through the 1920s, Moses remained active with the Idaho Democratic Party as a speaker and delegate to Democratic National Conventions. His last public appearance for the Democrats was on December 29, 1931.

Moses Alexander passed away on January 4, 1932. He is buried along-side his wife at the Morris Hill Cemetery in Boise.

Ahavath Beth Israel, built in 1896 in Boise, Idaho, is the oldest synagogue in continuous use west of the Mississippi. Though the community outgrew the building in 1998, it was decided to move the entire Rundbogenstil-style structure to a larger campus rather than abandon it. What looks like brickword is actually wooden shingles! *Photo: Louis Davidson.*

JOSEPH SIMON

JOSEPH SIMON was born in 1712, actual month and day unknown. He immigrated to the United States at the age of twenty-eight in 1740 and settled in Lancaster, Pennsylvania, from England. He became one of the first Jewish fur trappers and traders. In 1742, he moved out west and bought huge tracts of land, and became friends and business partners with William Henry, a gunsmith merchant. Simon was known as a worthy and honest man who was fair in his trading and dealing. After trading in the western Unites States for ten years, he relocated to the Susquehanna River area, which stretched from Maryland to New York. He traded furs and other necessities like pots and pans and tools with the Delaware, Shawnee, Iroquois, and Susquehanna Indian tribes along the river.

Simon passed away on January 24, 1804 in Lancaster, Pennsylvania, and is buried at Shaarai Shomayim Cemetery. At the time of his death, he was the last known colonial Jewish resident of Lancaster, Pennsylvania, due to most of the Jewish community moving to Philadelphia, Pennsylvania.

ALBERT EINSTEIN

ALBERT EINSTEIN was born March 14, 1879 in Wurttemberg, Germany. He became a theoretical physicist and graduated from the University of Zurich in 1905. In 1933, he began his journey to the western United States, just as Germany and Hitler were rising to power. Due to Albert's Jewish background, he did not want to return to Germany. Albert became an American citizen in 1940. On the eve of World War II, he endorsed a letter to President Franklin D. Roosevelt alerting him to the potential development of very powerful bombs and recommended that the U.S. begin to do research on this as well. Einstein supported the United States but thought nuclear weapons were very dangerous and hoped they would never be used in any type of war effort.

He sailed to New York 1930, where he celebrated Hanukkah with a huge party of fifteen thousand people at Madison Square Garden. He then traveled to California where he met Jewish actor Charlie Chaplin and became very good friends.

From there, he traveled to Arizona to see the Grand Canyon and was met by a group of Hopi Indians. Albert thought they were just local natives. He was also met there by Herman Schweizer, a past manager of the Harvey House and local trader. Mr. Schweizer was also there to translate for Einstein since he did not speak the Hopi's language. The Hopi planned to present Einstein with a headdress and make him an honorary chief of their tribe. Not knowing who Albert Einstein really was, they asked Mr. Schweizer. The following is actual dialogue.

"What's his business?" asked one of the Head tribesmen.

"He invented the Theory of Relativity," Mr. Schweizer replied.

"All right. We'll call him the Great Relative!"

Albert Einstein is mostly famous for his equation E=MC2. He also won the Nobel Prize in 1921 for his services to theoretical physics and for his discovery of the law of the photoelectric effect. The photoelectric effect is the emission of electrons or other free carriers when light hits a material. They are called photoelectrons. He received his award one year later in 1922.

Albert was also known as a phenomenal violinist. It was said that if he hadn't become a scientist, he might've been a famous musician.

He also loved to sail. While attending college at Polytechnic Institute in Zurich, Switzerland, he would often take his boat out on the lake, drop anchor and relax, think,

and write out his thoughts in his small notebook, which he carried everywhere. He never learned how to swim however he enjoyed sailing throughout his life.

Twenty-one years after writing his Theory of Relativity, Einstein invented a refrigerator that worked using alcohol gas. The appliance was patented in 1926 but never made it to production due to new technology.

Albert was a leader in establishing the Hebrew University of Jerusalem in 1925 and served among the universities first Board of Governors. He also suggested various courses creating an institute of agriculture in order to settle and work undeveloped lands in the west.

Albert Einstein passed away April 18, 1955. He died from an abdominal aortic aneurysm where he experienced internal bleeding caused by the aneurysm in Princeton Hospital at the age of seventy-six. He requested his body be cremated, but in bizarre incident during an autopsy his brain was removed and kept in the hope of unlocking the secrets of his genius.

DEADWOOD, SOUTH DAKOTA

THE DISCOVERY OF GOLD in the Black Hills of South Dakota started one of the biggest gold rushes of all time in 1874. Miners came from far and wide to pan for gold and lay claims to their personal mining properties. In 1876, Deadwood was born in the southwest corner of the Black Hills. The town was named for the area of dead trees and a creek full of gold. When viewing the town from a distance, the colors faded into a dark green and black upon the horizon. Deadwood was a town that had to set its own rules and laws because it attracted gunslingers, outlaws, gamblers, and miners. The miners had their own language, and here is a glossary of some of their slang.

- Buck out in smoke — man who died in a gunfight
- Butty — a fellow miner
- Cousin Jack — a man from a Celtic ethnic group from the United Kingdom, known as a Cornishman. Many came to the west for mining.
- Cousin Jenny — a Cornishman's wife
- Gospel Sharp — a preacher
- Mestang Court — a kangaroo court
- Powder Monkey — one who handles explosives
- River Sniper — a person who guarded the mines
- Rock Sharp — a mining engineer or geologist
- Rust eater — an iron worker
- Shack — mine guard
- Classifier or Grizzly – A screen or strainer to get rid of larger materials.
- Dredge – a common piece of mining equipment which sucks up dirt and gravel from within a stream by the use of water pressure.
- Dry Washing – Fine soil is blown away, leaving the gold.
- Stretch Hemp — to be hung by the neck
- Yellow Belly – Coward
- Yellow Hammer – Gold coin.
- Ten-Day miner — a miner who works part time
- The Colored Elevations — the Black Hills
- The miner's silicosis — a miner's lung disease from breathing the mine's air

- Tinhorn — a cheap and flashy man
- Tossing in another Grizzly — telling a tall tale
- Wife — a fellow working miner
- End Lines – the boundary of a miner's claim.
- Fathom – Six feet square on the vein.
- Vein – within the fissures of rock there are lots of mineral matter like gold and silver.
- Above Snakes – above ground and still alive.
- Ace in the Hole – A hideout or a hidden gun.
- All Beer and Skittles – Unpleasant, not so happy.
- Apple Jack – A liquor distilled from cider.
- Apple Pie Order – In top shape, perfect order.

Among the many who came to Deadwood to make their fortune were Wild Bill Hickock, Calamity Jane, Seth Bullock, Al Swearingen, and Solomon (Sol) Star.

Deadwood has survived three major fires, heavy rains, and mudslides. The town was revived in 1989 when gambling was once again legalized.

Today, Deadwood is a town with modern-day casinos, hotels, and spas.

The Gem Theater, said to be "an infamous den of prostitution under the guise of being a dance hall." *Centennial Collection, Deadwood Public Library.*

Miners and ore cars at the working face of an open cut in one of the many mines near Deadwood. The sheet-iron plates provide a smooth surface from which to shovel the broken ore. *Centennial Collection— Deadwood Public Library.*

Placer mining at Blacktail in 1908 was not much different from the gold rush of the 1870s; wet, dirty, backbreaking work. *Centennial Collection—Deadwood Public Library.*

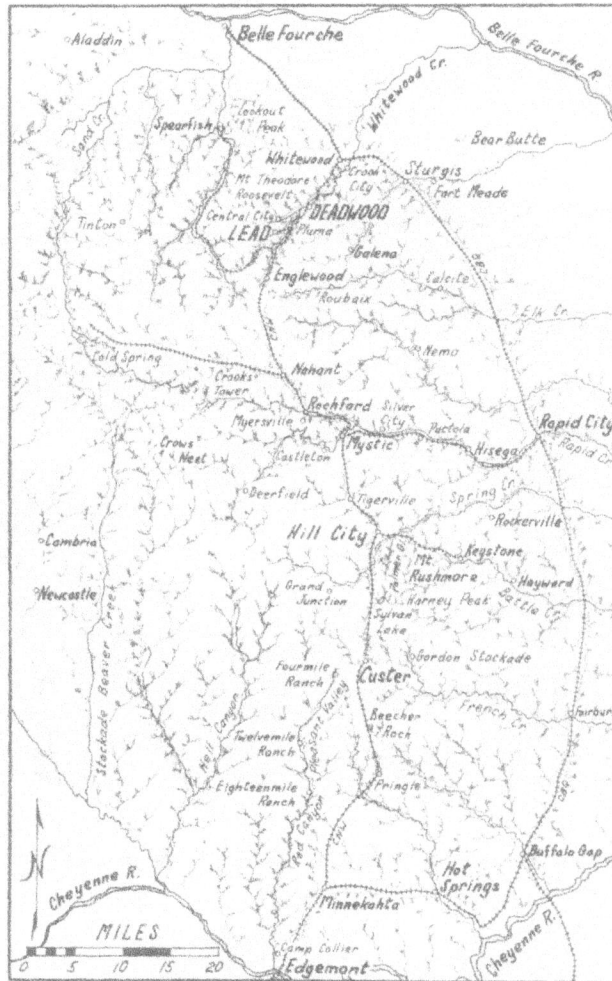

The Black Hills with their mining camps, stage stations, military posts, and a few of their many railroads.

Deadwood's men on Main Street, summer 1876

The Franklin Hotel has been a social center in Deadwood
since it opened in 1903. *W. Parker photo.*

Dredging on Whitewood Creek below Deadwood during the 1970s. *W. Parker photo.*

Ruins of the Belle Eldridge Mill in Spruce Gulch. *W. Parker photo.*

Dignitaries and old-timers ride in the Days of '76 parade each August in and upon the Deadwood stage. *Centennial Collection, Deadwood Public Library.*

Black Hills Pioneers—miners, businessmen, and other men who had arrived in the Black Hills before 1877

A SHORT GLOSSARY OF WESTERN & MINING SLANG

BUCK OUT IN SMOKE: die in a gun-fight

BUTTY: a fellow miner

COUSIN JACK: a Cornishman, many of whom were miners in the West

COUSIN JENNY: a Cornishman's wife

GOSPEL SHARP: preacher

MESTANG COURT: kangaroo court

POWDER MONKEY: explosives handler

RIVER SNIPER: placer miner

ROCK SHARP: mining engineer or geologist

RUSTEATER: ironworker

SAND: courage or pluck, from the Civil War phrase "plenty of sand in his crop"

SHACK: mine guard

SOILED DOVE: a prostitute

STRETCH HEMP: to be hanged by the neck

TAR BABY: cable lubricator

TEN-DAY MINER: itinerant miner

THE COLORED ELEVATIONS: the Black Hills

THE MINER'S: silicosis, a lung disease common among miners

TIGER: faro, named for the tiger painted on the faro box

TINHORN: a cheap and flashy man; a fake; a dude ex: "a tinhorn gambler"

TOSSING IN ANOTHER GRIZZLY: telling a tall tale

WIFE: fellow worker

SOLOMON "SOL" STAR

SOL WAS BORN TO JEWISH PARENTS in Bavaria, Austria, on December 20, 1840. At the age of ten, he was sent to Ohio to live with his uncle Abraham Frielander, who made a living as a garment merchant. Sol later moved to Helena, Montana, where he served as the territorial auditor and personal secretary to the governor.

While in Montana, he met and became best friends with Seth Bullock. They became business partners. In 1876, they moved to Deadwood to capitalize on the construction boom of the gold rush town. They purchased property from a hotel owner by the name of Al Swearengen and opened the office of Star and Bullock, Auctioneers and Commission Merchants. A commission merchant is someone who buys or sells products for a percentage of the sales price. They also formed a partnership in livestock ranching, calling their enterprise the S&B Ranch Company. The friends also contributed to further the economic development of the region by working with the Missouri Valley Railroad to build track to make Deadwood more accessible to other people and to make it easier to move livestock from one place to another.

They later built a hardware store on the main street of Deadwood. In 1894, the store and other businesses burned down in a raging fire. While the cleanup took place, the two decided not to rebuild their store. In its place, they built a luxury hotel called the Bullock Hotel.

Sol was the chairman of the first state Republican Convention. When South Dakota became a state on November 2, 1889, Mr. Star served as Republican senator.

A prominent member of Deadwood's large Jewish community, Sol was active in the local synagogue and contributed very generously to needy Jewish families in Russia and Europe. He was a respected and beloved public servant, politician, and businessman who helped bring prosperity to Deadwood.

Sol also owned a flour mill on upper Main Street. Estelline Bennett wrote, "As long as that mill was open and ground wheat, it was said that no one in Deadwood went without flour. Anyone in need could get a sack of flour at any time without money and without price. Those who could, paid for it at their convenience. Those who could not, never heard about it" — Estelline Bennett.

Sol never married and died at his ranch in Deadwood on October 10, 1917. His funeral was the largest and most extravagant ever held in Deadwood. His body was exhumed and later moved to St. Louis, Missouri, and laid to rest in the Jewish cemetery known as the Mount Sinai Cemetery and Mausoleum, opened in 1850. Today it is the oldest existing Jewish cemetery in St. Louis.

LETTER FROM SOL STAR TO BULLOCK

NOVEMBER 19, 1876

DEAR SETH:
Business as of old, is getting poorer daily as winter approaches. The stampede a failure (Wolf Creek). Many are the disgusted faces parading the streets of Deadwood.

The killing of a pilgrim, Shaunessey, by Dick Brown, a banjo picker, at Bella Union, November 10, and the killing of Farrell by Ed Cook are the only news worth relating. Farrell, you will remember, is the man getting logs for our roof who demanded pay from us and with whom you exchanged some

few words. I write more particularly at this time for the purpose of getting agency for the sale of blasting powder and giant powder."

YOURS TRULY,

Sol Star

Above, Star, center, and Bullock, right, in the 1880s.

SETH BULLOCK

SETH WAS BORN July 23, 1849 in Canada. As a young man, Seth was unhappy with life and finally left home at the age of eighteen. He was looking to find his own way in the world and make a name for himself. He arrived in Montana in 1867.

In 1867, Seth became a resident of Helena, Montana, and unsuccessfully ran for the post of Territorial Legislature. Later on, he was elected to the Territorial Senate as a Republican in 1871 and 1872. Seth helped to create Yellowstone National Park.

In 1873, Seth was elected sheriff of Lewis and Clark County, Montana. During his tenure, Seth killed his first outlaw named Clell Watson. Watson stole a horse and engaged Seth in a gunfight. Seth was shot in the shoulder but still took Watson into custody. On the day Watson was to be hanged for his crimes, a mob of people appeared and scared the executioner away. Seth then ran out and climbed the scaffold with a shotgun over his shoulder and pulled the lever himself sending Watson to his death. He then held off the mob with his shotgun.

Soon after, Seth reunited with his good friend, Solomon (Sol) Star. Together they opened a hardware store. It was a profitable business. However, the two men knew there was a big opportunity and untapped market for hardware in the gold rush town of Deadwood in the Dakota Territory. They moved to Deadwood and purchased a lot to build the store on and called it Star and Bullock Auctioneers and Commission Merchants.

At the time of their arrival Deadwood was a lawless and rowdy town. The day before, Wild Bill Hickock was gunned down by a gunman named Jack McCall, taking revenge for Hickock killing of his brother. The demand for law enforcement grew and Seth's background and reputation made him the perfect choice for sheriff.

Seth deputized several residents to help tackle the task of turning Deadwood into a civilized town. Due to Seth's reputation, he managed to make the town a better place to live without killing anyone. Having made Deadwood a safer town, Seth brought his wife, Martha Eccles Bullock, and daughter Margaret to town from Michigan. They later had another daughter named Florence and a son, Stanley.

Seth also was known for introducing the farming of alfalfa to South Dakota in 1881.

Seth met Teddy Roosevelt in 1884 while bringing a horse thief named Crazy Steve to face charges. They became lifelong friends. Mr. Roosevelt had said that "Seth Bullock is a true westerner, the finest type of frontiersman."

Seth and Sol purchased a ranch near Redwater Creek and the Belle Forche River and called it the S & B Ranch.

In 1884 Bullock and Star's hardware store had burned down. Rather than rebuild the store, they cleared the lot and started building Deadwood's first hotel.

The Bullock Hotel was built between 1894 – 1896. It was constructed and decorated in a Victorian style with the first floor having a large dining room, a large kitchen, and pantry. The was also a sample room where the salesmen could store their cases of goods. It was finished off with a grand lobby and offices in the front.

The second and third floors were known to have sixty-three luxury sleeping rooms with baths at the ends of the hallway and two large skylights for lighting the inner rooms with natural light. The rooms were also furnished with iron and brass beds and oak furnishings. The Bullock Hotel still stands today.

HAUNTING FOLKLORE

CONTRARY TO POPULAR BELIEF, Seth Bullock did not die at the hotel in room 211 but at his home at 28 Van Buren Street. It is possible that incorrect reports of his demise at the hotel propagated reports of his ghost being sighted at the hotel, which continue to this day by guests, workers, and tourists. Many people who have supposedly had contact with Bullock's ghost say that they were never harmed, but merely touched or called out for. Apparitions are often seen by guests and orbs of light as well. Orbs of light are spirits trying to manifest themselves. Employees say the ghost merely continues to "play host" and often makes sure "his" employees are working hard, because many employees have said when they were taking breaks, they felt paranormal presence, and got back to work immediately. Ghost tours of the hotel are held regularly, and many thrill-seekers, ghost hunting groups and non-believers have spent the night. In 2015, the hotel was featured on a special Halloween episode of Ghost Adventures.

Later in life, Bullock's friendship with Roosevelt led to his becoming a captain of Troop A of Grigsby's Cowboy Regiment. This was another volunteer calvary regiment which Congress authorized in 1898. The group was very similar to Roosevelt's Rough Riders.

When Teddy Roosevelt became vice president under William McKinley, Roosevelt appointed Bullock as the first forest supervisor of the Black Hills Reserve. After McKinley's assassination, Roosevelt became the youngest president of the United States at forty-two years old. He served from 1901–1909. In the inaugural parade of 1905, Seth hired fifty people to ride in the parade as security for the president. Soon after, Seth was appointed U.S. Marshall and served for nine years.

After Roosevelt's death in January of 1919, Bullock built a monument to him and dedicated it on July 4, 1919. The monument is located on Sheep Mountain and later renamed Mount Roosevelt.

Seth was known as a Canadian-American frontiersman, businessman, politician, sheriff, and U.S. Marshall.

Seth Bullock died of colon cancer on September 23, 1919 at his home in Deadwood. He is buried in Mount Moriah facing Mount Roosevelt.

BLANCHE COLMAN

BLANCHE COLMAN was the daughter of Nathan Colman and his wife, Amelia, Jewish immigrants who migrated to the west from Germany. Nathan and his wife came to Deadwood in 1877 and opened a tobacco store. In 1878, Nathan was appointed a justice of the peace and served as a rabbi for the Jewish population of Deadwood.

Judge Nathan Colman and his daughters Blanche and Theresa circa 1905.

In 1884, Amelia Colman gave birth to the first Jewish baby to be born in Deadwood. They named her Blanche.

Blanche grew up around the mines where her father worked part-time, learning all she could about the business. After graduating high school in 1902, she went to work for Congressman William Parker as his secretary in Washington, D.C. She later returned to Deadwood to work in the legal department of the Homestake Mining Company. She started as a clerk and advanced through the ranks to a legal assistant. She studied hard, night after night in the office of her boss, Chambers Kellar, Esq.

On October 3, 1911, Blanche became the first female admitted to the South Dakota Bar Association. As a lawyer, she worked on many mine-related cases that dealt with labor disputes and negotiations and water rights. In 1950, Blanche became a well-respected lawyer and started her own practice, which she had until her death in 1978.

Blanche Colman opened the door for many more women to become lawyers among other positions in law firms throughout the United States.

JAMES BUTLER (WILD BILL) HICKOCK

WILD BILL HICKOK was a sharp-dressing sharpshooter who was both tough as a nail and a nice guy. He killed as many as thirty-six outlaws over the course of his career. Wild Bill was an American folk hero of The American old west best known for his work as a wagon master, soldier, spy, scout, lawman, gunfighter, gambler, and actor.

He was born May 27, 1837 and raised on a small farm in northern Illinois. He grew up and lived a ruffian lifestyle. At age eighteen, he headed west. He worked as a stagecoach driver and later as a lawman in Kansas and Nebraska. During the Civil War between the North and South, he fought and acted as a spy for the Union Army, which supported the North.

On August 2,1876, he was sitting at a table with his back to the entrance of the bar playing poker in a Deadwood local saloon called Lewis and Mann No. 10. While playing his hand, a lowlife gunman named Jack McCall walked in and shot Wild Bill in the back of the head instantly killing him. He blamed Hickok for killing his brother and wanted revenge. Wild Bill's final poker hand is now known as the dead man's hand, consisting of two pairs, black aces and eights.

He was buried in Deadwood's Ingleside cemetery. However, in 1879, his remains were exhumed and reburied in Mount Moriah Cemetery in the Jewish section just outside of Deadwood. No one knows what his religion was, but to be moved from Ingleside cemetery to a Jewish plot in Mount Moriah cemetery does throw light on the fact that he might have been Jewish.

"Calamity Jane" Cannary Burke and the photographer pose in front
of Wild Bil Hickok's grave around the turn of the century.
Centennial Collection, Deadwood Public Library.

Jack McCall, the murderous nobody who shot Wild Bill Hickok
from behind in Nuttall and Mann's Saloon No. 10, 2 August 1876.
Centennial Collection, Deadwood Public Library.

The real Charlie Utter, right, posing with Wild Bill Hickok's tombstone and an unknown friend, soon after Bill's grave was moved to Deadwood's Mt. Moriah cemetery

Y FRIEND, WILD Bill, remained in Deadwood during the summer with the exception of occasional visits to the camps. On the 2nd of August, while setting at a gambling table in the Bell Union saloon, in Deadwood, he was shot in the back of the head by the notorious Jack McCall, a desperado. I was in Deadwood at the time and on hearing of the killing made my way at once to the scene of the shooting and found that my friend had been killed by McCall. I at once started to look for the assassin and found him at Shurdy's butcher shop and grabbed a meat cleaver and made him throw up his hands; through the excitement on hearing of Bill's death, having left my weapons on the post of my bed. He was then taken to a log cabin and locked up, well secured as every one thought, but he got away and was afterwards caught at Fagan's ranch on Horse Creek, on the old Cheyenne road and was then taken to Yankton, Dak., where he was tried, sentenced, and hung.

—CALAMITY JANE, "LIFE AND ADVENTURES OF CALAMITY JANE, BY HERSELF"

JIM LEVY

JIM LEVY was born in Dublin, Ireland, in 1842 to Jewish parents. He migrated to the western territory as a young man. He first came to Nevada and worked as a miner in 1860. In 1871, he found his calling as a gunfighter.

On May 30, 1871, Mr. Levy was outside the Midnight Star Saloon and witnessed two men having a heated argument. One of the men, Mr. Mike Casey, pulled his pistol and shot Mr. Tom Gasson in cold blood. Mr. Gasson survived but stayed bedridden and offered five thousand dollars to any man to avenge his shooting. At Mr. Casey's trial, Jim Levy was called to testify as an eyewitness to the shooting. Jim testified that Mr. Casey was the first to fire his gun.

Later, Casey caught up to Levy and challenged him to a gunfight. Levy left to get a weapon and faced Casey in a back alley to square off. Levy fired first and the bullet hit Casey just grazing his skull. He fired again this time hitting him in the neck. Levy was charged for murder but was acquitted claiming self-defense. He also claimed the five-thousand-dollar bounty.

Realizing that he could make more money as a hired gun than a miner, he changed from a gunfighter to a gun for hire. He also made his living as a professional gambler on the side. He moved from town to town, living in Cheyanne, Wyoming; Deadwood, South Dakota; and ending up in Tucson, Arizona, after leaving Tombstone.

On March 9, 1877 in Cheyanne, Wyoming, Jim Levy was playing cards in The Shingle and Locke's Saloon. He got into another heated argument, this time with a man named Charlie Harrison. The two met out in the street for a classic western shootout. Harrison drew first but missed. Levy drew and fired one shot. Charlie Harrison fell to the ground, dead as a doornail. Levy was taken to jail and awaited trial. Again, he claimed self-defense and was acquitted.

In Tombstone, Wyatt Earp and Bat Masterson were reading their newspapers which referred to Mr. Levy as a "pistoliferous gambler." Wyatt knew Jim Levy and Bat Masterson had praised his skill as a gunfighter. Wyatt Earp had always said, "Take your time but be in a hurry." Levy always believed speed was fine, but accuracy was final.

Levy fought and survived sixteen shootouts. On June 5, 1882, Mr. Levy was drinking and gambling in the Fashion Saloon in Tucson and was unarmed, meaning he did not have his guns with him. In the early hours of the morning, he left the saloon and was ambushed by a local group of rivals and shot dead. No one knew why he did not carry his gun that day. A gun for hire always carried his gun.

TOMBSTONE, ARIZONA

TOMBSTONE, ARIZONA was the home of Wyatt Earp, his brothers, and Doc Holiday, along with Josephine Marcus. Ms. Marcus was the Jewish wife of Wyatt Earp. Tombstone had a long history of Jewish settlers who were prospectors and merchants and, yes, even cowboys. There were even Jewish lawyers and statesmen. Enough Jews lived in Tombstone to create the Tombstone Hebrew Association in 1881. One of their first orders of business was to create and dedicate a corner of the municipal cemetery to be a Jewish burial ground within the Boot Hill Cemetery.

In 1882, a local historian invited a Jewish economist, Israel Rubin to tour the neglected and rundown Jewish burial site. Along for the inspection was local community leader Judge C. Lawrence Huerta, a Yaqui Indian From Tucson. Mr. Rubin recited the Kaddish, a Jewish prayer to remember the dead. Judge Huerta was so inspired that he made a promise to restore Boot Hill's Jewish area and rededicated the site in 1884. A plaque now proclaims that the site is "Dedicated to the Jewish pioneers and their Indian friends" and contains a bowl of earth brought in from Jerusalem, now resting with Arizona's earliest Jewish settlers.

Another Jewish businessman was A.H. Emanuel, the superintendent of a company called the Watermill Mining Co. A.H. Emanuel came to Tombstone in 1880. Besides the mining company, he also ran a blacksmith and wagon shop out of the same warehouse. Later in 1896, he was elected as mayor of Tombstone and served till 1902.

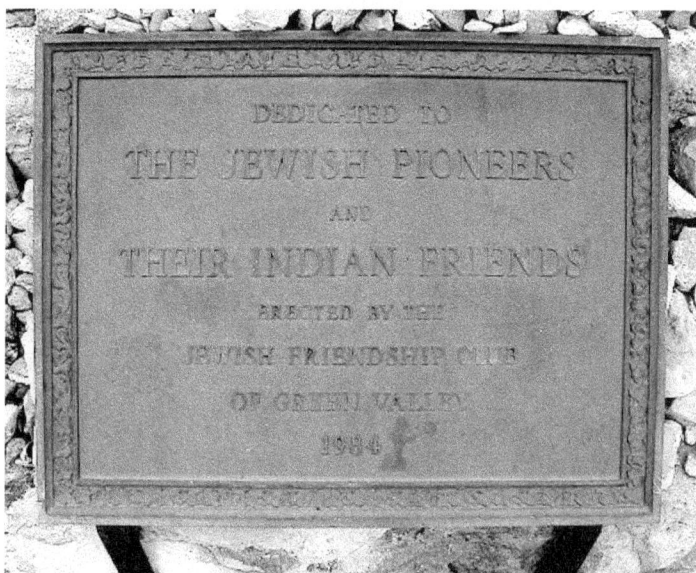

The Cochise County Bank was also set up and owned by Lionel M. Jacobs and his brother Barron Jacobs. Other businesses like the R. Cohen hardware store were set up and run by Jewish clerks. There were also tobacco companies, mercantile and jewelry stores, barbershops, and tailor shops run by Jewish businessmen in Tombstone.

There were only two businesses that were known to be operated by

Jewish women. Mrs. David Gotthelf operated a French millinery shop, and Mrs. H. Cohen managed a high-end fancy dry goods store.

Between 1881 and 1883 and estimated four hundred to five hundred Jews came to Tombstone to grab their opportunity for success. A synagogue was never built in the town, but it is recorded that Jews did use a building for their services.

HERMAN BENDELL

DR. HERMAN BENDELL was born in Albany, New York, on October 28, 1843. He was an American physician during and after the American Civil War. He entered the service in the New York Volunteer Infantry Regiment as a hospital steward in 1861. He served with the Sixth regiment New York Heavy Artillery as an assistant surgeon. Then on February 19, 1863, he became lead surgeon with the Eighty-Sixth regiment New York Volunteer Infantry.

In furthering President Ulysses S. Grant's peace policy, Dr. Bendell was appointed superintendent of Indian affairs for the Arizona Territory. He was considered the first Jew to settle in the city of Phoenix. He arrived shortly after the infamous Camp Grant massacre. His first order of business was to accompany General Oliver Otis and members of various Indian tribes and the first Apache delegation to Washington, D.C. The five chiefs were: Antonio Azul, Pimo Chief; Louis Mohnjo, Pimo interpreter; Ascension, Papago Subchief; Josio Pakato, Apache Zuma; and Carlos, the Apache Mohave.

This was a very troubled time in the Arizona Territory. The United States government wanted to move the Apache tribes to reservations with a farming lifestyle. Dr. Bendell's report stated the tribe's reluctance to accept the conditions offered by the U.S. government and that the Native Americans were hoarding rations for the purpose of carrying out attacks on the settlers taking over their land. After the treaty for The Arizona Territory was finally signed, Dr. Bendell was chosen by Apache Chief Cochise as a supporting officer. In the words of Dr. Herman Bendell in 1872, "I feel it a duty that I owe to the people of the country, and the Indians under my charge, to do something to relieve the pressures that surrounds them, and earnestly solicit the Department to accord to me a discretionary power in the matter."

Bendell would often visit all the tribes to discuss their

needs. He obtained good, low local prices for government contracts and supervised the receipt of supplies and ensured they were given to the Indian tribes. The Board of Commissioners praised Dr. Bendell's accomplishments. However, they still recommended he be replaced by a Christian. Bendell served as the last Jewish superintendent of Indian affairs in the Arizona Territory. He served that office from 1871–1873.

Bendell returned to Albany, New York, and married Wilhelmine Lewi in 1873 and had four children.

Dr. Bendell passed on November 14, 1932. He is buried in the Bet El Emeth Cemetery in Albany, New York.

"CURLY-HAIRED WHITE CHIEF WHO SPEAKS WITH ONE TONGUE"

ON MAY 30, 1854, President Franklin Pierce signed the Kansas-Nebraska Act which officially defined the territories of Kansas and Nebraska and opened up a major part of what would become the Wild West. Many Jews settled there, including merchants and traders.

Julius Meyer was born in Prussia in 1851 and moved to Omaha, Nebraska as a teenager in 1866 to join his brothers in trade. It was said that Meyer was captured by Ponca People and was saved from being scalped by Chief Standing Bear who saw a greatness Meyer. This relationship would allow Meyer to make his mark on the world and on the Wild West.

Meyer felt very comfortable among the different tribes and became fluent is six different tribal languages. This also helped his interactions with the local Native Americans which helped build his business and curio shop called The Indian Wigwam. He respected the tribes and took a special interest in them, which set him apart from many of the other settlers. The Indian people were always welcome in his store, and Meyer always treated them like friends. The local Chieftain gave him the name Box-Ka-Sha-Hash-Ta-

Ka which translates to "Curly-Headed White Chief with One Tongue." One tongue was given to him in honor of Meyer's honesty, for a person with one tongue could not speak out of two-sides of his mouth.

Meyer also served as both an interpreter for the Native Americans to congress and as an Indian agent for the government.

The records also stated that Meyer was involved with both the first synagogue in Nebraska, Congregation of Israel of

Omaha, now called Temple Israel, and Omaha's Hebrew Benevolent Society. In 1886, Meyer also founded the Young Men's Hebrew Association in Omaha, which sponsored social and literary entertainment.

After many years of active participation in civic and Jewish affairs, Julius Meyer was found dead in Hanscom Park on May 10, 1909.

Wolf Kalisher: An Ally of Native Americans

WOLF KALISHER was born in Poland in 1826. Kalisher moved to Los Angeles, California, in 1855 and became a United States citizen. When the Civil War ended, he became partners with Henry Wartenberg, opening-up a tannery, one of the first factories in the city in 1871. A tannery is a place for treating skins and hides of animals to produce leather and getting the leather ready for use in making belts, shoes, jewelry, and other clothing.

He quickly became an ally to the Native Americans. He hired many Native American workers and worked hard to protect their rights. He also became widely known as a man who developed the L.A. community by investing in the city establishing one of the first synagogues called Congregation B'nai Brith in 1862. He married his wife, Louise, and had four children. Louise was the founding president of the Ladies' Hebrew Benevolent Society. Today, it is known as the Wilshire Boulevard Temple.

He became close with a leader of the local Temecula tribe named Manuel Olegario. He advised and assisted the chief as he worked to protect his tribe's land in San Diego County. Wolf died in 1899. Los Angeles memorialized Wolf Kalisher and his efforts on behalf of the Native Americans naming a street after him which still bears that name today.

THE ORTHODOX PIONEERS OF COTOPAXI

SOUTHERN COLORADO was a harsh, rocky, and desolate terrain, certainly an unlikely site for a settlement of Yiddish-speaking Orthodox Jews. However, in 1882, very religious immigrants from Tsarist Russia moved to Cotopaxi, Colorado, hoping to start a Jewish agricultural colony.

In the spring of 1882, a young Jewish immigrant from Russia named Michel Shames brought his wife and two young children to the United States. They boarded a train in New York City and travelled five days to Colorado. The Shames family were joined by a dozen other Russian-Jewish families which included Michel's father and two of his younger siblings, all hoping for a better life and the freedom to observe the Jewish religion. Their dream was to find a Jewish agricultural colony and prove themselves as successful farmers. The colony grew to more than twenty-two families with more than sixty men, women, and children.

When the travelers arrived, they were greeted with curiosity and some suspicion by local residents, who had never seen Jewish people before. The men wore kippot, small skullcaps, on their heads and had tallit strings hanging out from beneath their coats called tzitzit. The married women wore long frontier dresses with head coverings such as hats, scarves, and wigs. Michel's brother-in-law, Philip Quiatkowsky, had taught himself English before leaving Russia and was able to communicate with the locals.

Amongst the Jewish farmers were former grain merchants, carpenters, a tailor, a barkeep, and a Hebrew teacher. They were ready and prepared to take up plows and hoes and learn how to farm. However, they were not prepared for the harsh winters and had very limited supplies. They also built bonfires at night to keep the bears away from their supplies and cabins.

In the 1870s, the town had begun to attract a few settlers and mining prospectors.

By the 1880s, Cotopaxi was a small town with only two hundred residents and a dozen businesses.

One of the first Jewish colonists at Cotopaxi was a teenager named Yudel (Ed) Grimes. In his later years, he recalled his experience and said, "Cotopaxi was the poorest place in the world for farming. The land was poor, there were lots of huge rocks and basically no water. The few crops that we were able to raise by a miracle were mostly eaten by cattle, which belonged to neighboring settlers."

The prospect of making a living was so bad after the first year that Mr. Grimes walked a hundred and fifty miles to Denver, where he worked for a dollar a day and saved enough money to bring eight family members to America.

In 1881, a well-known local Cotopaxi Jewish businessman by the name Emanuel Saltiel contacted the representatives of the German-Jewish-run Hebrew Immigrant Aid Society in New York and convinced them that Cotopaxi could be turned into a paradise of farming land if the Jewish immigrants were willing to work the land.

Between 1880 and 1890, it was approximated that two hundred thousand Jews came from Eastern Europe to the United States, most of them from Russia and Poland. The Jewish community welcomed the immigrants who had fled their homelands because of persecution and poverty. However, the German Jews were worried that the new immigrants with their embarrassing "Old World" traditions would promote anti-Semitism and threaten their middle-class status. Therefore, in support of Jewish agricultural endeavors around the U.S., the German Jews removed the Russian Jews from crowded urban areas on the East Coast, mostly from New York City, and moved them around the country attempting to Americanize them a lot faster. This worked very well in getting the Jewish to be more American.

At the start of 1881, nearly twenty-five Jewish agricultural colonies were established in various locations throughout the U.S. to the immigrants who had been denied the right to own land in Europe.

Few of these colonies made it. The Hebrew Immigrant Aid Society officials had hoped that the Cotopaxi people would become self-supporting farmers.

By the year 1884, an immigrant by the name of Shul Baer Milstein came to Cotopaxi, and then Denver, and became a founder of Congregation Zera Abraham and built a successful cattle business.

The HIAS met with Jacob Milstein, who had arrived from Russia in 1878 to work out the details for the support of the project. Jacob was the nephew of Shul Baer Milstein. Shul Milstein realized that there was little hope for Jews in Russia due to the severe economic, religious, and social discrimination against the Jews. So, his nephew, Jacob was sent ahead to America to scout out the opportunities for the Jewish people.

He met with Emanuel Saltiel of the HIAS, and the site offered appeared to be a good match for the Jewish immigrants. Saltiel promised to procure the land for the new settlers, build houses, and supply the immigrants with everything they needed to succeed. HIAS put out nearly ten thousand dollars to set up the Jews in Cotopaxi.

Shortly after arriving in Cotopaxi, some of the men traveled by horse and wagon to inspect the sites of their future homes. Their inspection would be the first of a list of major disappointments. The finished homes turned out to be a total of eight poorly constructed cabins, with no windows, chimneys, or furniture. Not only that, but there were only four stoves for all twenty-two families. And the stream the farms were built near was dry for most of the year.

Of the 1,780 acres the Cotopaxi colonists were given, only a few hundred were fit for cultivation and these acres needed extensive irrigation. Horrible weather, natural disasters, rocky land, no experience with high-altitude farming, and the meager supplies and farming implements hindered the colonists from the start. The only crop they ever produced on the land was a poor harvest of potatoes. The colonists also dealt with food and fuel shortages. Desperate for money, several of the men turned to temporary jobs in Saltiel's mines. They worked hard all day to earn $1.50 in pay. Others later earned three dollars daily working as railroad workers with the Rio Grande Railroad. They were very happy working for the railroad because the company allowed them to work on Sundays instead of Shabbat.

RELIGIOUS LIFE IN THE COTOPAXI COLONY

DUE TO THE DRY SOIL and rocky terrain in Cotopaxi, the farming was doomed to fail. But the religious aspects and life in the community were as strong as ever. The non-Jewish people of Cotopaxi had just constructed a brand-new schoolhouse and offered its use for Shabbat services to the Jewish colonists. Later a cabin was constructed and served as a synagogue. It was named B'nai Shalom. A request was made to the HIAS for a Torah. The Torah arrived on June 23, 1883. The Torah was received with a joyous festivity. The New York Jewish Messenger described the ceremonies:

"At 5:30 pm a procession was formed as follows: First marched the elders of the colonists, each one holding a candle in his hand, then came a chuppah, the four poles carried by four single men, and later came the women and children. The procession then entered the synagogue and several psalms were sung, the Russians chanting the familiar melodies which so deeply move the Jewish heart."

Two Passover seders were conducted while the Jewish colonists lived in Cotopaxi. One seder was presided over by the scholarly Hebrew teacher, David Grupitsky, who served as the cantor and rabbi of the community. The colonists also requested and received kosher meat and matzah from Denver, Colorado, which they added to their own baked matzah. The kosher food received was also considered kosher for Passover. They used flour they obtained by walking twenty-six miles to the small town of Salida. The generous Jewish community of Denver, less than five hundred people at the time, provided whatever they could to the colonists of Cotopaxi which included financial aid, food, and clothing.

By June of 1884, nearly two years after the settlement was first established, the colonists were forced to disband. The colonists were unable to farm the land given to them and most had moved to Denver. Some colonists still pursued farming and moved to Derby and Broomfield, Colorado, and other places in the American west.

Even though the colony of Cotopaxi was unsuccessful, it did help shape a group of Jewish leaders who would make major contributions to Jewish life in the American west and would help the Jewish community thrive in the region. The colony of Cotopaxi gave the colonists experience interacting with their new Gentile neighbors and valuable exposure to the American culture, as well as civic and political life.

Shul Baer and his wife, Miriam, arrived in Denver in 1884 and built a very successful cattle business. Their daughter Nettie and her husband, Jacob, farmed near Broomfield, where they and their nine children lived for many years without running water or indoor plumbing. The children went to school in a one-room schoolhouse several miles from their home either arriving by foot or on horseback. The family finally sold their farmland to the Savory Mushroom Company during the Depression for the sum of $18,000.

Many of the Cotopaxi colonists who settled in Denver became peddlers, junk dealers, and small shopkeepers. Some became successful business owners and community leaders.

Yudel (Ed) Grimes, the seventeen-year-old who walked all the way to Denver, became one of the founders of Denver's West Side Orthodox Congregation. The synagogue was incorporated in 1889 and is still in existence today. Mr. Grimes was also an organizer of the Moshev Zekanim Society, which later came to be the Beth Israel Hospital and Home for the Aged. He became their first president in 1918.

Yudel was also a very successful businessman. However, he never forgot his humble beginnings. He often gave newcomers jobs and accompanied them to city hall to help them obtain citizenship papers.

Even though the colonists of Cotopaxi had very rough times, their experience became a success story. Had the colonists stayed in Russia, many of their family members and descendants would have perished in that harsh region, particularly later during the Holocaust.

The colonists, through their courage and perseverance, helped forged new and productive lives in the West. They formed the nucleus of what was to become Denver's West Side Jewish Community.

The information in this section comes from Jeanne Abrams, a professor at the University of Denver and longtime director of the Beck Archives and the Rocky Mountain Jewish Historical Society.

JEWISH CONGREGATIONS

IN 1851, Lewis A. Franklin moved to San Diego, California, and organized the first services for the High Holy Days in Southern California. By 1852, Franklin's congregation bought land on Stockton Street and asked for donations from the settlers and property owners to build their own synagogue in which to worship. Franklin received plenty of donations, and by 1853 their synagogue was built. They soon had 110 individual and family memberships, mostly immigrants from Northern Europe and England. The congregation was a strict Orthodox synagogue. Orthodox Judaism is a major branch within Judaism that teaches strict adherence to rabbinical interpretation of Jewish law and its traditional observances. The new synagogue was named Sherith Israel.

In 1854, a temple was established in San Francisco, California. It was called Congregation Emanu-El. It was different from Sherith Israel as it was a Reform synagogue. A Reform synagogue practices a form of Judaism initiated in Germany by the philosopher Moses Mendelssohn (1729-1786), which has reformed or abandoned aspects of Orthodox worship and ritual in an attempt to adapt to modern changes in social, political, and cultural life. The rabbi was Dr. Cohen who was originally from Germany where the Reform movement got its start. This congregation had 260 members, comprised mostly of German Jews and French natives.

Today, California has one of the largest Jewish-American populations of about one million. The main Jewish communities are found in Los Angeles and the San Francisco Bay area. Also, Russian Jews today are migrating and settling in urban communities such as Sacramento and Palm Springs.

Wherever Jews went, cities grew, and synagogues were built. From 1852–1854, four more synagogues were founded in the west. Only ten pre-1912 synagogues still stand west of Louisiana and the Mississippi. Seven still remain in use today. All ten of them can be viewed inside and out. Together they constitute the last visible remains of the Jewish Wild West.

•••

Jewish merchants were crucial to western expansion. Their businesses were often the spark that turned a remote little town with no more than a bar and stable for horses into a thriving and bustling town. The Jewish pioneers were so successful that by 1900 there wasn't a single settlement west of the Mississippi which had not had a Jewish mayor, including Deadwood, Tombstone, and Dodge City.

LEON DYER

LEON DYER was born in Alzey, Germany on October 2, 1807. He was originally named Feist Emanuel Heim. He was the son of John M. Dyer who was the first president and organizer of the Baltimore Hebrew Congregation.

Leon immigrated to Baltimore, Maryland, with his family in 1812. He spent part of his young life working in his father's meat-packing business, which was reported to be the first kosher plant in America.

In 1834, when riots broke out, the mayor was reported to be out of town. Dyer took command, hiring people and lawmen to help restore order.

Dyer went to visit New Orleans to help promote and drum up business for his father's meat-packing business. It was here that Dyer accepted the job of quartermaster for the state militia. As quartermaster, Dyer was a senior soldier who supervised stores and/or barracks and distributed supplies and provisions, as well as clothing and food for the soldiers. In quartermaster position, he fought in the Mexican War, the Seminole War, and the War of Texas Independence. He served as a major in the Seminole War under General Winfield Scott and again under Scott from 1845–47 in the Mexican War. Dyer played a major part in clearing bands of plundering Mexican troops from west Texas. He even escorted the captured Mexican general Santa Anna to Washington D.C.

When he returned to Baltimore, he was elected president of the Baltimore Hebrew Congregation in 1840 and served till 1845. In 1848, Dyer was promoted to Colonel and crossed the mountains and plains to California. There between 1849 and 1850, he helped to organize the first service for the High Holy Days at San Francisco's Kearny Street Congregation.

In 1852, he married and went on to have four children.

He passed away September 14, 1883. He is buried in Galveston, Texas at the Hebrew Benevolent Society Cemetery.

WOMEN WHO HELPED SETTLE THE WILD WEST

MS. FLORA LANGERMAN married a Jewish-American pioneer named Willie Spiegleberg in 1874 and settled in Santa Fe, New Mexico. She started a Jewish school for the eight Jewish children who lived in her town. Her husband became the first Jewish mayor in 1884 and held the position for two years.

One morning Flora heard the cries of a young slave woman outside her bedroom window. The slave girl, Flora found out had been kidnapped by confederate soldiers during this Civil War period. The girl's name was Emily. Flora brought the girl into her home and proceeded to wash the girl and feed her. She gave her clean clothes and then sent for a doctor to make sure Emily was healthy. Flora's doctor was a man who believed everyone should have good health care, so he agreed to come and see the girl. Flora adopted Emily, and soon after, Flora and Emily helped two other captives, a Native American brother and sister who came to their home as well. Flora and her husband adopted the pair and raised them as their own children.

JOSEPHINE MARCUS EARP

JOSEPHINE MARCUS was born in 1861 in New York City, New York, to parents Hyman Marcus and Sofia Lewis. Hyman Marcus arrived in New York around 1854, escaping political and limited opportunities in Posen, Poland. It was here that he met Sofia and married her in 1855. They had three children Nathan, Josephine, and Henrietta.

Josephine was interested in acting and theater. At age eighteen, she left her Jewish life behind and went to San Francisco, California, to take music and dance classes. She enrolled as a voice student under the coaching of Mrs. Hirsch. She learned a lot of music by Gilbert and Sullivan, which happened to be the music of the era. She then joined the Markham Pinafore on Wheels troupe and performed to capacity crowds throughout the Arizona territory. By December of 1879, her group of singers and actors had reached Tombstone.

The Markham Pinafore on Wheels disbanded on January 28, 1880. Josephine contacted her parents and told them that she wanted to come home. While back in San Francisco, Sheriff Behan came to see her and propose marriage. Josephine turned him down.

A year earlier, Wyatt Earp and his brothers Virgil, Morgan, and James along with their wives arrived in Tombstone on December 1, 1879. He became good friends with Bat Masterson. At the time, Bat Masterson was a deputy in Tombstone. At the same time, Wyatt Earp had his eyes on Josephine and began seeing her. The two of them hit it off and became inseparable. At the beginning of 1881, Josephine went back to San Francisco to visit her family.

When Wyatt's days in Tombstone were over, he went to San Francisco in mid-1881 to meet up with Josephine and continue their lives together.

Wyatt and Josephine left San Francisco to go to Utah where they met Bat Masterson and his wife with whom they remained good friends. At dinner one evening, Bat explained Wyatt's actions in Tombstone to Josephine. He told her that "Wyatt was like a hardworking housewife who hated dirt and uncleanliness in his home, meaning outlaws and people intent on breaking the law." Josephine fully understood.

In 1882, Josephine and Wyatt left for Colorado and then to Idaho to explore the silver fields. They had to cross the eleven- thousand-foot Red Mountain Pass which was still covered in snow. Wyatt suggested that she wear overalls over her clothes for warmth. Stylish as she was, Josephine fought this idea, but soon realized that Wyatt was right, and she wore the overalls along with a heavy coat, scarf, and gloves. When they arrived in Colorado, Wyatt met a Jewish merchant named Henry Jaffa. The merchant replaced Wyatt's long coat which was full of bullet holes from his previous gunfights in Tombstone, Arizona.

Note: Wyatt never took a bullet to his body.

The couple went their separate ways in 1883 to attend to personal matters and family. Wyatt went to Dodge City, Kansas, and met up with Bat Masterson to work on the Dodge City War and Peace Commission. Josephine went home to San Francisco for her sister Henrietta's wedding to her Jewish husband Emil Lenhardt, who was a businessman who sold goods to the people of San Francisco.

Reunited with Wyatt in December of 1883, Josephine married him and started using the name Mrs. Earp.

Next, the two moved to San Diego, California, when his brother Virgil contacted him. Wyatt always put his brothers first when they came calling which most of the time was to help bring a dangerous outlaw to justice.

Once in California, Wyatt judged horses and refereed fights at the Escondido Fair.

Josephine loved horse racing. Wyatt owned several horses many of which were very successful at the track. Some of his winnings went to buying expensive jewelry for Josephine. They travelled the racing circuit, and Wyatt rode many a horse to victory. As his ownership of horses grew, he hired some of the best jockeys around. They all wore the Earp racing colors, navy blue dots on a white field.

Toward the end of 1894, Wyatt and Josephine made their way back to San Francisco, so she could be closer to her family. Her father became ill and passed on January 5, 1895. He was the first of the Marcus family to be buried in The Jewish Hills of Eternity Cemetery.

The two of them left San Francisco in 1898 and finally made it to Alaska to get away from Wyatt's turmoil and his reputation of a lawman in his Tombstone days.

Wyatt Berry Stepp Earp passed away January 13, 1929 at eighty years of age. Josephine did not attend Wyatt's funeral because she felt it was a day for the public to mourn. Wyatt Earp was cremated. Six months later, Josephine travelled back to San Francisco and buried his ashes next to her father in their family owned plot in the Hills of Eternity Cemetery.

Josephine's last years were spent with her family living a quiet life. She died December 19, 1944. No one attended her funeral as she had detached herself from the Jewish religion many years before. Josephine was cremated and laid to rest in her family plot next to Wyatt Earp, her beloved. They had been married for forty-seven years.

MARY GOLDSMITH

MARY GOLDSMITH was one of the first Jewish women to migrate to California following the gold rush of 1849. At the age of five, Mary arrived in San Francisco by way of steamship from Poland with her family.

Mary's father became active in Sherith Israel congregation. Her family joined other Jews in celebrating the High Holy Days, Rosh Hashanah and Yom Kippur. Rosh Hashanah is known as the Jewish New Year. Yom Kippur is known as the Jewish Day of Atonement.

Because this was an Orthodox congregation, the men occupied the main floor while the women were seated in the gallery. Mary observed that when the Jewish people were away from their homes, family and friends clung a lot closer to each other. They were very devoted to their faith.

Mary grew up to become a respected teacher in religious and public school. She worked hard and became a high school principal and the first Jewish female member of the San Francisco Board of Education. Mary passed away in 1935.

On March 4, 1925, Mary's daughter Florence Prag Kahn became the first Jewish congresswoman in the United States. Florence was born November 9, 1866 in Salt Lake City, Utah, and died November 16, 1948 in San Francisco, California. She served in the House of Representatives in a seat left vacant by her husband Julius Kahn. She was the first woman to serve on the House Military Affairs Committee. She served until January 3, 1937. After serving in Congress, Kahn actively tried to get women involved in politics. She was a member of the American Association of University Women, Hadassah, and the Council of Jewish Women. She was a member of Emanu-El of San Francisco, which is a Reform synagogue.

BLANCHE COLMAN

BLANCHE COLMAN was the daughter of Nathan Colman and his wife Amelia, Jewish immigrants who migrated to the west from Germany. Nathan and his wife came to Deadwood in 1877 and opened a tobacco shop. A few months later, Nathan was elected justice of the peace and served as a rabbi for the Jewish population of Deadwood.

In 1884, Amelia Colman gave birth to the first Jewish baby to be born in Deadwood. They named her Blanche.

Blanche grew up around the mines where her father worked part-time, learning all she could about the business. After graduating high school in 1902, she went to work for Congressman William Parker as his secretary in Washington, D.C. She later returned to Deadwood to work in the legal department of the Homestake Mining Company. She started as a clerk and advanced through the ranks to a legal assistant. She studied hard, night after night in the office of her boss Chambers Kellar, Esq.

On October 3, 1911, Blanche became the first female admitted to the South Dakota Bar Association. As a lawyer, she worked on many mine-related cases that dealt with labor disputes and negotiations and water rights. In 1950, Blanche started her own practice which she had until her death in 1978.

Blanche Colman opened the door for many more women to become lawyers among other positions in law firms throughout the United States.

The women in the west served as the guardians of Jewish benevolent societies and institutions in Jewish orphanages, hospitals, and homes for the elderly.

NANETTE CONRAD BLOCHMAN

NANETTE CONRAD BLOCHMAN (Yiddish name – Yettel) was born in Bavaria in 1830. She came to America with her family and first settled in New York City before moving to San Francisco, California, in the mid-1850s. She met and married Emanuel Blochman, a Jewish pioneer and scholar who had arrived in San Francisco in 1851 from Alsace-Lorraine.

With the help of the gold rush of 1849, San Francisco was a growing city and in the mid-1800s was the site of the region's largest Jewish population.

Mrs. Blochman was a businesswoman who operated a number of millinery shops. She was a strict follower of the Jewish faith and kept her shops closed on Saturdays as well as the Jewish holidays. She was sometimes the main provider for her family. Her husband instituted a Torah school for children in 1864. He also worked as a dairy farmer, made wine, and baked matzahs for Passover, which celebrates the exodus of the Jewish people out of Egypt to free themselves from the slavery under the Egyptian rule.

The family belonged to Congregation Ohabai Shalom. Nanette was a notable example of a pious woman who always observed the traditions of old Israel and making sure the kosher dietary laws were constantly followed.

•••

By the late 1800s, Denver, Colorado, was also a growing city with a large population of Jewish people. Many of the Jews coming to Denver arrived from the Russian agricultural colony of Cotopaxi. Other Jews migrated to Denver for health and economic opportunities. Colorado had a reputation for being the world's sanitorium due to its high altitude and dryer air for those seeking a cure for tuberculosis.

Denver's west side became a traditional Jewish enclave filled with many small synagogues, as well as kosher bakeries, butcher shops, and grocery stores.

MIRIAM KUBESKI

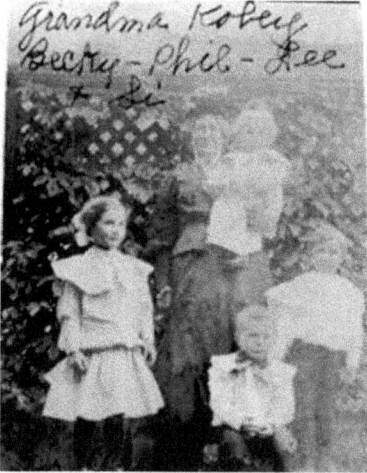

IN THE MID-1880S, Miriam Kubeski, her husband Abraham, and their children migrated from England to Central City, Colorado, which was becoming a booming silver mining town.

Miriam was born in Suwalk, Poland, and given the name Miriam Rachofsky. Her husband became a very successful merchant in Central City. He formed a minyan in a storefront and even acquired a Sefer Torah. A minyan is a minimum of ten people needed to have a prayer service. A Sefer Torah is a handwritten copy of the Torah which contains the five books of Moses. His brother served as the rabbi for years to come.

In 1888, Miriam, now going by the name Miriam Kobey, because it was easier to say, moved to Denver and became a midwife. Her husband, Abraham, helped establish the Agudas Achim synagogue and earned a modest living as a rabbi. In 1901, Abraham ordered matzahs from Manischewitz. When they failed to arrive in time for Passover, he enlisted the help of the town blacksmith and built an enormous oven behind the synagogue. There, he baked his own matzahs for the Jewish community.

Miriam was doing quite well as a midwife. She earned the nickname Denver's Angel of Mercy, due to her concern for the poor people in the community. She also delivered some babies for no charge to those who could not pay. Miriam also asked for donations and baby clothes to help the poor. And she would always bring her delicious chicken soup to the new mothers.

Her granddaughter gave her the name the Pied Piper of West Colfax, referring to the main street that ran through Denver's Eastern European town. It was said that when Miriam was spotted wearing her famous white cap, a spotless apron, and carrying a black bag prepared with birthing implements, she was always joined and followed by a group of children. She had delivered many of them. She was also thought of as a surrogate grandmother.

She and her husband were founders of Denver's Jewish Free Loan society. Their family name has been at the forefront of philanthropy in Denver for nearly one hundred years.

Miriam passed away in 1921.

Upon the arrival of the Jewish immigrants in the United States, many Jewish women with names beginning with an "M" sound took the common English name of Mary.

CONGREGATIONS IN THE WEST

IN 1848, the first synagogue west of the Mississippi was built in St Louis, Missouri. Then the gold rush established the towns of Sacramento, Stockton, and San Francisco. This is where the next four synagogues were founded between 1852 and 1854.

Lewis Franklin moved to San Diego, California, in 1851 to organize the first service for the High Holy Days. In 1852, Franklin's congregation used donations from the settlers to buy land on Stockton Street to build their own synagogue. By 1853, the temple was built. They soon had 110 members, mostly immigrants from northern Europe and England. They were a strict Orthodox temple, and it was named Sherith Israel.

In 1854, a temple rose up in San Francisco, California called Emanu-El. It was different than Sherith Israel as this was a Reform synagogue. The rabbi was Dr. Cohen, who was originally from Germany where the Reform movement actually got its start. This congregation had 260 members, made up mostly of German Jews and French natives.

Today, California has about one million Jews and is one of the largest Jewish-American populations in the United States. The main Jewish communities are found in Los Angeles and the San Francisco Bay area. Also, Russian Jews coming over from Russia today are settling in urban communities such as Sacramento and Palm Springs.

BIBLIOGRAPHY

Jeanne Abrams, professor at Penrose Library at the University of Denver and longtime director of the Beck Archives and the Rocky Mountain Jewish Historical Society.

Bennett, Estelline. *Old Deadwood Days*. Lincoln and London: University of Nebraska Press, 1982.

Brener, David A. The Jews of Lancaster, Pennsylvania: A story with two beginnings. Lancaster: Congregation Shaarai Shomayim, 1979.

Fried, Steven *Appetite for America: Fred Harvey and the Business of Civilizing the Wild West--One Meal at a Time*. New York: Bantam Books, 2011.

Appetite for *America: How Visionary Businessman Fred Harvey built a railroad hospitality empire that civilized the Wild West (Bantam, 2010)*

Isaacson, Walter. *Einstein: His life and Universe*. New York: Simon and Schuster, Reprint Edition, 2008.

Libo, Kenneth, and Irving Howe. *We Lived There Too: In Their Own Words and Pictures Pioneer Jews and the Westward*

Movement of America 1630-1930. New York: St. Martin's Press, 1985.

Reiss, Oscar. *The Jews in Colonial America*. Jefferson, NC: McFarland & Company, 2004.

Rischin, Moses, and John Livingston. *Jews of The American West*. Detroit: Wayne State University Press, 1991.

Rochlin, Harriet, and Fred Rochlin. *Pioneer Jews: A New Life in the Far West*. Boston: Houghton Mifflin Harcourt, 2000

Sharfman, I. Harold. *Jews on the Frontier: An Account of Jewish Pioneers and Settlers in Early America*. Malibu, CA: Pengloss Press, 1991.

Weiser, Kathy. *Legends of America*. Old West Lawmen, updated July, 2015

The Western Jewish History Center in Berkley, CA. *Manuscripts of Mary Goldsmith, Norton B Stern*, 2007

Whittaker, E. *Albert Einstein. 1879 – 1955. Biographical Memoirs of Fellows of the Royal Society.*. (November 1, 1955)

References

^ Jump up to: a b c d *Shadley, Mark; Wennes, Josh (September 4, 2012).* "The Bullock Hotel". *Haunted Deadwood: A True Wild West Ghost Town. Arcadia Publishing Incorporated. pp. 60–63.* ISBN 978-1-61423-675-7.

^ "U.S. Marshals Service, History, United States Marshal Seth Bullock". *Usmarshals.gov. Retrieved July 18, 2012.*

^ Jump up to: a b c *Wolff, David A. (2009).* Seth Bullock: Black Hills Lawman. *South Dakota State Historical Society Press. pp. 11–14.* ISBN 978-0-9798940-5-3

^ *McClintock, John S. (1939).* Pioneer Days in the Black Hills: Accurate History and Facts Related by One of the Early Day Pioneers. *University of Oklahoma Press. pp. 166–167.* ISBN 978-0-8061-3191-7.

^ *Stasi, Paul; Greiman, Jennifer (December 20, 2012).* The Last Western: Deadwood and the End of American Empire. *Bloomsbury Publishing. pp. 33–34.* ISBN 978-1-4411-2652-8.

^ Seth Bullock. 1893 Theodore Roosevelt Birthplace National Historic Site. http://www.theodorerooseveltcenter.org/Research/Digital-Library/Record.aspx?libID=o283087. Theodore Roosevelt Digital Library. Dickinson State University.

^ Jump up to: a b c d *Dary, David (2007).* "Who was Seth Bullock?". *True Tales of the Prairies and Plains. University Press of Kansas. pp. 117–120.* ISBN 978-0-7006-1518-6.

ABOUT THE AUTHOR

EDWIN M. RADIN is a Jewish author who lives in Columbus, Ohio. He writes stories for children, teens, and young adults. His works include The Reluctant Penguin series, a trio of books teaching young children lessons in life and how to achieve their goals.

He has also written an autobiography about his fourteen years in a Jewish Scout troop called *The Troop Clown*, filled with stories and pictures of beautiful places he has travelled to as a Scout.

His first novella is called *Gersham and the Golem*. A great story taking place in the mid-eighteenth century in Southern Poland with a Bal Shem and his five students learning the Kabbalah which was written up in *The Columbus Jewish News*.

He is currently working on a new project called *How the Jews Settled the Wild West* with stories and pictures of the Jewish people who helped make the west what it is today.

You can find his books on Amazon and Amazon International along with Barnes and Nobles.com, iTunes, and Koho.com.